TR
BT

D1113710

Does a Lobsterman Wear Pants?

Does a Lobsterman Wear Pants?

And 184 Other Questions
You've Always Wanted to Ask about
Lobsters and Lobstering

ANSWERED BY

BARBARA DELINSKY

DRAWINGS BY ROB GROVES

 Down East Books

ISBN 10-digit: 0-89272-679-2

ISBN 13-digit: 978-0-89272-679-0

LCCN: 2004117295

Cover design by Phil Schirmer

Book design by Lurelle Cheverie

Printed at Versa Press, E. Peoria, Ill.

5 4 3 2 1

Down East Books

A division of Down East Enterprise, Inc.

Publisher of *Down East,* the Magazine of Maine

Book orders: 1-800-685-7962

www.downeastbooks.com

Contents

Author's Note

Do I do research when I write a book? Oh boy, do I ever! I research before the writing, during the writing, and sometimes even after the writing to make sure that my facts are correct. The thing is, though, that most of what I learn on any given topic is for my own understanding of the matter at hand. Precious little of it appears in the actual book.

And that's how it was writing my novel *The Summer I Dared*. For the sake of creating a realistic lobsterman in the protagonist, Noah Prine, I had to learn all I could about his world. As a result, I had reams of information on lobsters and lobstering, all heading into storage, never to be seen by the rest of the world. The thought of that broke my heart. In the course of my research I did run across small collections of lobster trivia, but there was nothing that came close to what I had in my files.

So here are the things I found. To call them trivia is something of a misnomer. Some of what follows is indeed pure fun, but more of it is interesting bits of information focused on the rugged life of the Maine lobsterman and his eight-legged "bug."

This collection is by no means exhaustive; you may have more to add, particularly if you hail from areas other than Maine. Nor is everything that is printed here the law. Lobstering is not an exact science; there were times when I found confusing—even conflicting—information. I've tried to sort it all out as best I could. And I've tried to simplify, hence some absolute-sounding answers, but I suspect I've still made mistakes. Please forgive those and know that my intentions were pure—pure and heartfelt, because I love Maine. Indeed, lobstermen capture the ruggedness and independence that is quintessentially Maine.

Okay, though. I confess. I also feel an affinity for lobstermen because I love eating lobster.

I was nine when I ate my first one. I was at summer camp, and it was lobster night. To this day, I don't know whether the counselors were tutored beforehand in the art of eating lobster. There we were, a table of seven nine-year-old campers, and one twenty-something counselor, trying to pick and pull and crush to get our meal. Actually, one of the seven campers had wimped out and ordered tuna salad, but I wouldn't have dreamed of doing that. Lobster night happened only once a summer. It was a tradition at my camp; I wanted to partake.

Did I prefer the claws or the tail? The tail. Back then. And now. It wasn't until I turned fourteen that I had anything other than boiled live lobster at camp. To commemorate that particular birthday, my dad took us to the venerable Boston restaurant Locke-Ober, and I had Lobster Savannah. Yummm. In subsequent years, at other restaurants, I had Lobster Thermidor, baked stuffed lobster, lobster stew, lobster crepes, grilled lobster, and, of course, lobster salad.

I was an adult before I tried cooking lobster myself. Actually, I was adult enough to be a mother, and the only other person in the family interested in making boiled live lobster was my son, Andrew, a high schooler at the time. Both lobster lovers, with no one else home for dinner that night, we thought cooking our own was a *fabulous* idea. In high spirits, we went to the fish market and bought two live lobsters. Our spirits lowered a tad after we had arrived home and dumped them into the sink, and realized that they were, uh, truly alive. Then came the pot of boiling water. Let me tell you, that was it for me. I can't kill things. We did eat those lobsters that night, but with zero enjoyment. Neither of us has ever boiled a live lobster since then.

I buy lobster already cooked. Call me a wimp, but that's how it is. I buy it cooked and then do something with it—such as mixing it into salad with diced celery and mayonnaise just barely diluted with fresh lemon juice, or heating it in Newburgh sauce. My favorite recipe is the simplest, given to me by my friend Keith Marden, owner of Captain Marden's Seafood in Wellesley, Massachusetts, where I buy all my fish. It's kind of a lobster stew, Nova Scotia style, according to Keith, and calls for heating cooked lobster meat in butter and adding half-and-half to taste. That means if I want it stew-y, I add more; if I want it over rice, I add less. Whichever way I do it, it tastes fresh and delicately flavored, and it's good.

Let me end by telling you one more story. This one's about my maternal grandfather. He was a barrel maker whose business was on the waterfront in Portland, Maine. As a child, I used to visit him there. I remember dark wooden barrels with metal rims, pieced together in a cavernous stone building that smelled of the sea. Mostly, though, I remember the man himself. He was tall and well built, though he stooped some with age, and he had huge hands. But he was gentle. He used to come to our house, sit my sisters and me on the piano bench beside him, and play "Let me call you sweetheart, I'm in love . . . with . . . you. . . ." I did love him, too, which is very possibly why I also love waterfronts, salt air, and sea smells.

This wee book, which does capture waterfronts, salt air, and sea smells, has taken me back. . . .

Truly yours,
Barbara Delinsky

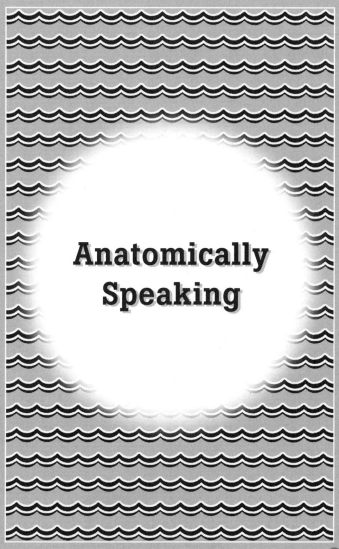

Anatomically Speaking

How do lobsters breathe?

Taking air from the water, they "inhale" through their legs and "exhale" through their heads. The actual breathing is done by gills, which extract oxygen from the water as it moves from legs to head.

Do lobsters have teeth?

No. They swallow meat whole and let their stomachs do the chewing.

Do lobsters hear?

Not as we do. But some lobstermen believe that lobsters go into hiding on July 4 as a result of the noise of fireworks. This surely explains any empty traps on July 5.

Do lobsters have eyes?

They do, but those eyes don't see very well. They are best at monitoring movement, alerting the lobster to the presence of another sea creature. As for identifying what that creature is, the antennae and the sensitive little hairs on the lobster's legs are better at doing that than the eyes.

Can lobsters smell?

Yes, yes, yes! They have large and small antennae, but it is the small ones, called antennules, that serve as a nose. A flick of those antennules is comparable to a sniff. Lobsters depend on their sense of smell for successful mating. They also depend on it for locating food. This sense of smell is one of the things that draws a lobster to a baited trap. Curiosity is the other. Put any new object near a lobster and it will investigate posthaste.

Do lobsters have blood?

They sure do. It's a clear fluid that turns red when it hits the air and becomes an opaque whitish gel when cooked. It is tasteless and safe to eat.

Do lobsters bleed when wounded?

Yup. Sometimes a newly wounded lobster will start to bleed when it is hauled to the surface. Because the water pressure on the ocean floor helps stop the bleeding, the lobsterman may put this lobster back in the trap, lower it again, and pull it up another day.

How many body segments does a lobster have?

Twenty-one.

Can lobsters regenerate missing limbs?

Yes. Not only can they regrow legs, claws, and antennae, they can part company with these same parts in order to escape danger. Lobsters have even been known to drop a claw for no reason at all. A lost claw will regrow in six to eight weeks, though it is generally smaller than its predecessor.

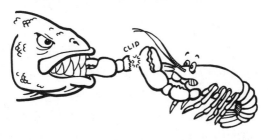

Where are lobsters found?

There are different kinds of lobsters in different parts of the world. The North American lobster, or

Homarus americanus, is found along the East Coast of North America from Newfoundland to North Carolina. Maine is the largest lobster harvesting state. Her waters, whose temperatures are better suited to the lobster's anatomical needs, supply 50 percent of those lobsters caught for food.

What do lobsters eat?

Crabs, mussels, clams, flounder, starfish, urchins, and the like. Because lobsters are meat eaters, toxins in the water do not enter their flesh as would be the case if they were filter feeders, as are clams and mussels. Lobsters are therefore safe to eat even during an outbreak of red tide.

How fast can a lobster run?

A lobsterman claimed to have caught and released a lobster, then recaught the same one a day later, three nautical miles away. On a regular basis, lobsters are thought to travel a mile on the ocean floor in a single night in search of food. Legend has it that one tagged lobster was tracked from Penobscot

Bay to Cape Cod, for a total of 138 miles in a single year. Not bad on eight spindly three-inch-long legs.

How big is the largest lobster ever caught?

The Massachusetts Lobstermen's Association claims that a lobster measuring 2.1 feet in length and weighing 37.4 pounds was caught off Cape Cod in 1974. A Maine lobsterman claims to have caught a lobster that was 3 feet 6 inches long and weighed more than 40 pounds. Divers working off the coast of Maine claim to have seen lobsters estimated to be 200 pounds. Wisely, they kept their distance, so we'll never know for sure.

How long can a lobster live?

Rumor has it that, during the 1700s, lobstermen found lobsters that were 150 years old. But scientific studies didn't begin until the 1800s; the oldest lobster on record was 100 years old and weighed 43 pounds. Of course, the word "scientific " may be relative here. The fact is that a lobster regularly sheds the one thing that might tell us its age—its shell. Lacking that, and any sort of backbone or spinal column, there is no way of knowing for sure how old a lobster is unless it lives those scores of years in captivity, where it can be watched.

A lobster isn't really red down there in the ocean, is it?

Most aren't. They're blue green, mottled brown, and olive green.

What's a half-and-half?

A lobster that is split in color, with one side one color and the other side another.

What's a calico?

A lobster whose coloring is marbled black and orange yellow.

How rare is a blue lobster?

Very. Blue coloration is found in only one in 2 million individuals.

What makes a blue lobster blue?

The same thing that makes an albino lobster white; it's a genetic condition.

How much of their weight do adult males carry in their claws?

Up to 50 percent.

Is a lobster right handed or left handed?

Hard to tell. One claw is usually larger; this is the crusher claw. The other is the tearer claw. Once in a while you find a lobster with two crusher claws and no tearer, or vice versa.

What is the pincer, or pincher claw?

Same thing as the tearer, or tearing claw.

What is a one-pound lobster called?

A chicken, or a chick.

What is a deuce?

A 2-pound lobster.

What is a "select" lobster?

One that is between 1.75 and 3.5 pounds.

What is a lobster born without claws called?

A crayfish.

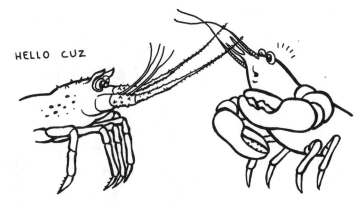

HELLO CUZ

What is a lobster that has lost one claw called?

A cull.

What is a lobster that has lost two claws called?

A pistol.

If a lobster is a short, what is it?

Too small, legally, to be taken from the sea.

What's a snapper?

Same thing as a short.

What should you do if you find a short in your trap?

Toss it back into the ocean.

What is the correct way to toss it?

Tail first. This pushes water through the gills in the proper direction for breathing.

What's a shedder?

A lobster during the molt stage, when its shell is new and soft. A shedder fetches a lower price on the market; it contains less meat because the lobster hasn't fully grown into its new shell.

What's a keeper?

A lobster that is of legal size for harvest. Also called a counter.

How long does it take for a lobster to grow to legal size?

Six years on average.

What is legal size?

In Maine, a lobster must be a minimum
of 3.25 inches and a maximum of 5 inches,
when measured from the eye socket to where
the body meets the tail.

What do lobstermen call a young lobster?

A young lobster. Only an unabridged dictionary
calls it a lobsterling.

What is the carapace?

The shell covering the body. It contains the brain,
heart, and stomach, all of which are inedible.

How big is a lobster's brain?

Roughly the size of a grasshopper's.

 28

Do lobsters feel pain?

Because their brains are little more than a tiny ball of nerve endings, if they do feel pain, it certainly doesn't register the way it does in humans.

Can a lobster scream when boiled alive?

Lobsters have no vocal cords.

How do you minimize the risk of traumatizing a lobster when putting it in boiling water?

Put it in the freezer for a few minutes. The cold numbs those nerve endings. Once in the pot, it'll be cooked before it knows what's hit it.

What does a lobster do when it is agitated?

Produces a vibrating sound, something like a very low bee buzz. Humans can't hear it, but other marine creatures sure can. If the vibrating takes a predator by surprise, the lobster can escape.

How do you calm an agitated lobster?

Support its body by cradling it under the legs.

How do you separate two lobsters that are gripping each other?

Submerge them in water, and they'll usually let go.

How do you hypnotize a lobster?

Hold it head down and rub its back. It will stay in this position without moving.

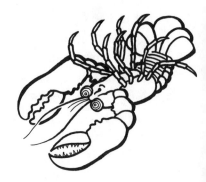

How often does a lobster shed its shell (molt)?

Up to four or five times a year. If it takes six years for a lobster to reach legal size, that means anywhere from twenty-four to thirty molts.

What is the purpose of the molt?

Growth. With each molt, the lobster increases its size by about 20 percent.

What happens to the old shell?

Sometimes the lobster eats it himself. This is for the sake of the calcium, which then helps the lobster's new shell harden.

NEEDS PEPPER

How does a lobster molt?

The shell splits up the back, and the lobster just backs away from it.

How long does the molt take?

Half an hour.

When one shell comes off, is there another already there beneath it?

Yes, but the new one's a softie, more like a gelatinous sheet. It takes upward of six weeks for it to properly harden. During this period, the lobster is vulnerable to predators and usually hides on rocky bottom (a good Maine expression) until it has the protection it needs.

Romantically Speaking

How do you tell a male lobster from a female?

Lobsters have small, feathery appendages, called swimmerets, on the underside of the tail. The first pair closest to the body on a male is hard and bony; on a female, this first pair is soft and feathery, as are the others.

Why is the tail on a female lobster wider than that on a male?

It protects all the eggs she carries. How much wider is it? Oh, somewhere in the 10 percent range.

Is the male the aggressor in the mating game?

No. The female goes looking for the biggest, strongest male she can find. The alpha male lobster? You could say that.

Are there names to differentiate male and female, like bull and sow?

Nope. They're both called lobsters. For the sake of the discussion, let's call them Lady and Lance.

So, how does the mating work?

It's actually kind of sweet. Lady is able to mate only right after she molts. So, just prior to the molt, she approaches Lance's den and releases a sex scent, which he brings into his den by fanning the water with his swimmerets. Then he emerges from the den with his claws raised, and there may be a brief boxing match. When she is ready to mate, Lady shows her submission by putting her claws on his head. They enter the den and, anywhere from a few hours to a few days later, she molts. This is when the mating takes place. Lance is quite gentle. He turns her onto her back and does his thing. She may remain in his den for a week after that while her new shell hardens. He protects her during this vulnerable time. Then she ups and leaves without a backward glance.

Is there monogamy among lobsters?

Sorry, but no. A male will mate with as many females as approach his den. Studies in which multiple females are in a tank with a single male have shown that the females time their molt to occur before or after the molt of another female. Technically, as soon as one female molts, mates, and leaves the male's den, another female that is ready to molt will approach.

What happens when multiple males are put in a tank with a single female?

They cannibalize one another. Most lose at least one leg. The female is so horrified by the violence that she may put off her molt until there is a clear victor, or until someone takes pity and gets her out of the tank.

How many eggs does the female produce?

On average 10,000. Large females have been known to produce 100,000 eggs at a time.

How long is she "pregnant"?

Once she expels the eggs, she carries them attached to her body, under her tail, for ten months. She can prolong this or speed it up, depending on living conditions on the ocean floor.

How does she care for these eggs she carries?

First and foremost, she protects them from predators. She also does daily aerating and cleaning of the eggs.

Of 10,000 eggs that hatch, how many grow to become lobsters big enough to harvest?

About ten.

What happens to the other 9,990?

Barely the size of a pinhead when hatched, they are eaten within a month by other fish as part of the food chain. Cod love lobster larvae.

How do those ten survive?

They sink to the ocean floor and hide among the rocks.

What's a berried lobster?

A female with fertilized eggs attached to her outer body. It is illegal for lobstermen to take berried lobsters. Rather, they return them (gently) to the sea.

What's a seeder female?

Same as a berried one: a female with eggs under her tail. Also called a breeder or an egger.

If a female is "egging out," what is she doing?

Extruding fertilized eggs and attaching them under her body.

What's a notched lobster?

When a lobsterman brings up a berried lobster in a trap, he often cuts a small V-notch in one of her tail fins. If another lobsterman brings up this same female at a later time, when she has no attached eggs, the notch tells him that she is of good breeding stock, so he returns her to the sea to breed again.

How long does it take for the V-notch to grow out?

Two years of molts, give or take.

What is a V-notched lobster called?

A bitch.

Historically
Speaking

41

Where did the word lobster come from?

Likely from the old French *loppe,* meaning spider. Lobsters have five pairs of legs. The front pair grows into claws. The back four pairs are used for travel and to grasp food.

Historically, what medicinal uses were lobsters thought to have?

Lobster meat was considered a diuretic. Same with the broth of boiled lobsters. Other parts of the lobster were used to treat urinary diseases, eye inflammations, and epilepsy.

Is a lobster really a water insect?

You could say that. Lobstermen often call a lobster a "bug." Formally, a lobster is an arthropod. Other arthropods include insects, spiders, and centipedes.

So what's a crustacean?

Any member of the large class Crustacea, which includes arthropods such as lobster, crab, and shrimp.

How long have lobsters been around?

Lobster fossils have been found in 511-million-year-old limestone deposits in England. Ancient Romans depicted lobsters on their mosaic floors.

What is the earliest mention of lobster in the history of America?

When Governor William Bradford reached Plymouth, Massachusetts, with a group

LOBSTER? AGAIN!

of settlers in 1622, he was embarrassed that supplies were so short that lobster had to be eaten.

Did Native Americans eat lobster?

Don't know for sure. Word is, though, that lobster was so plentiful that they used it to bait their fishing hooks and fertilize their fields. In Colonial America, lobsters were given to widows and children as charity, and to prisoners and indentured servants as lowly fare. During the occasional uprisings, servants insisted that it be put in their contracts that they wouldn't have to eat lobster more than three times a week.

I SAAAY...

When did eating lobster come into favor?

During the nineteenth century, when European royalty took a fancy to it.

How was the earliest lobstering done?

Until the early 1800s, lobsters were picked by hand out of the live rockweed that washed onto the shore.

What kind of boat did early Maine lobstermen use?

Rowing dories, which had high sides, a flat bottom, and a pointed bow.

And after dories?

Peapods. Ayuh, that's right. With a pointed bow and stern (called double-ended) and rounded sides, they looked like, well, the veggie. More stable than the dory, the peapod could be rowed in either direction, giving the lobsterman greater flexibility. The peapod was also said to hold a larger catch than the dory, though shape more than size was the greatest distinction between the two. Both boats could be fitted with a sail.

And after peapods?

The Friendship sloop. Believe it or not, these single-masted boats were built for lobstering before they ever became pleasure craft. They had a forward cabin that made cold-weather lobstering easier, and they were bigger than the dory or the peapod, hence could hold a larger catch. All this, and still one man could handle the gaff-rigged sails and haul traps himself!

What's a smack?

A sailboat used in the earliest days of commercial lobstering to carry lobsters long distances. Smacks had tanks that circulated seawater so that the lobsters stayed alive through the trip. This concept predates the modern lobster pound, in which lobsters may be kept alive until the market price rises.

When did commercial lobstering begin?

In Maine, in the 1840s. The season was four months long then, starting on March 1 and ending on the Fourth of July.

What gave lobstering the single largest boost?

Canning, the method of preserving food in airtight containers, which was developed in the mid-1800s. This made it possible to preserve lobster for long periods of time. Lobster fishing burgeoned as a direct result of this.

What precipitated the birth of the modern lobster boat?

The invention of the small gas-powered engine, giving the individual lobsterman reliability and speed.

What makes a lobster boat different from other boats?

Its bow is high and pointed, while its stern is low, flat, and wide. Such a stern makes it easy to stack lobster traps and get them in and out of the boat.

What is the modern lobster boat made of?

Traditionally, lobster boats were made of wood, but the trend now is toward fiberglass. Fiberglass boats are usually lighter than wood, so the fisherman uses less fuel. They are also faster, increasing the lobsterman's productivity. Moreover, upkeep is easier with fiberglass.

After whom does a lobsterman traditionally name his boat?

An important woman in his life.

How long is a lobster boat?

It can range anywhere from a 12-foot punt to a 120-foot offshore lobster boat.

What is the lobster shift at the local newspaper?

The predawn shift, so called because that's when lobstermen head out to work.

If someone is "lobsterish," what is he?

Red faced.

What's a lobsterback?

A Redcoat, or British soldier in his red uniform, so named by the American soldiers during the Revolutionary War.

Occupationally Speaking

What hours does a typical lobsterman work?

Predawn to late afternoon, often 4 a.m. to 4 p.m.

Why so early in the a.m.?

The water is calmer earlier in the day. Calmer water makes for easier fishing. By the time the seas get rough, the lobsterman likes to be heading home.

What does he have for breakfast?

As much of whatever as whoever can make.

What are oilskins?

Foul-weather gear, such as overalls, aprons, and jackets. Nowadays, they're made of rubber or PVC-coated cotton. Originally, they were made of cotton that was treated with linseed oil, hence the name.

Are oilskins always yellow?

No. They may instead be orange, green, or white.

What are Grundens?

Oilskins made by a company called Grunden. The name is spelled out on the wide suspenders.

Does a lobsterman wear pants under his oilskins?

Mais oui. At least, he says he does . . .

Does a lobsterman ever go bare chested under his Grundens?

Rarely. The suspenders would chafe his nipples.

What's a boot band?

An elastic strap that goes on the outside of the oilskin legs at the shin or ankle. The boot band holds the pants tight to the boots underneath and prevents water from splashing up inside.

Does a lobsterman wear shoes under his boots?

No way. If he falls overboard, he wants to be able to slip free of his boots and be as unencumbered as possible.

Does a lobsterman wear gloves?

When he's hauling traps, always—cotton in summer, insulated rubber in winter. In the old days, he wore felted wool mittens, and he actually wore them wet, because they were warmer that way. Brrr.

What's a sou'wester?

An oilskin hat with a large back brim that prevents water from going down the lobsterman's neck.

What is a lobster pot?

Same thing as a lobster trap.

How big is a lobster trap?

There are 3-footers and 4-footers, plus a few sizes in between.

What are lobster traps made of?

They used to be made solely of wood. Nowadays, many lobstermen prefer traps made of plastic-coated heavy-duty wire. These are more sturdy and longer lasting and require less maintenance than wood.

What's this thing about different "rooms" in a trap?

There are actually two. The lobster swims along the ocean floor and enters the first room through a funnel-shaped net called a head. This room is called the kitchen, because it is where the bait bag hangs and the lobster eats. Of course, he can't turn around and go out, because the inside end of the net is too narrow. So, compounding his error, he goes through a second one-way head into the parlor, or bedroom, where he is stuck. Here he sits until the lobsterman takes him out.

What are funny eyes?

The metal rings on the narrow end of the head that keep the net funnel shaped.

And the bridle?

A short length of strong, thick rope that is attached to the trap at each end to make sure that it surfaces evenly. The pot warp, the rope that connects the trap to the buoy, is tied to the bridle.

What keeps a lobster trap on the ocean floor?

Bricks. Seriously.

How many traps is a Maine lobsterman allowed to set?

Eight hundred.

How many traps are attached to a single buoy?

Anywhere from one to fifteen. Two is the norm.

What does it mean to fish strings?

It means that the lobsterman uses many traps that are connected by rope and set in a line on the ocean floor, with a buoy on the surface to mark each end.

What is a buoy made of?

It used to be made of cedar, but that was heavy when wet. Nowadays, a buoy is made of plastic or Styrofoam.

How much does a buoy cost?

$5 and up, depending on size, material, and features. Fancy ones can cost more than $50. The average cost is $7 to $15.

How long does a buoy last?

That depends. The three greatest threats to buoys are poachers, who cut them off; boats, whose props mangle them; and—in the case of Styrofoam buoys—seagulls, which eat them.

Why are buoys painted?

To make them easy to see, and to identify their owner. Every Maine lobsterman is required to register his colors on his lobstering license and put his license number on each buoy. He is also required to display one of his buoys in a visible spot on his boat, usually near or atop the pilothouse.

Are there other identifiers?

Sure are. Every trap a lobsterman sets has a metal tag attached to it. This tag shows his lobstering license number, as issued by the state of Maine.

How much does a wire lobster trap cost?

$55 to $63.

What is the average life span of a wire trap?

Four years.

How many traps does a lobsterman stand to lose in a bad storm?

Easily half, possibly all of his stock.

What's a ghost trap?

A trap that's lost on the ocean floor when the line tying it to its buoy is severed.

What happens to lobsters stuck in ghost traps?

By law, every trap must have a panel held on by biodegradable clips, called hog rings. When they disintegrate, the panel falls open and the lobster is freed.

What is an escape vent?

A small opening in the trap that allows undersize lobsters to walk in and walk out.

Do lobstermen work seven days a week?

According to Maine law, lobstermen are not permitted to haul pots on Sundays from June 1 to August 31, except if a big storm is brewing, in which

case they may go out to move their traps to deeper water, away from rocks.

What months are the most productive for lobstermen?

August and September.

Are there bad months for lobstering?

In a way. Lobsters generally molt at the beginning of June and the end of December. During the six to eight weeks following the molt, they are soft shelled and contain less meat, hence bring in less money.

Do lobstermen work through the winter?

Some do. The work is harder and takes longer, though, because traps have to be set in deeper water, farther from shore, where the lobsters go to escape the cold. Conversely, though, some lobstermen fish only in winter; because the market supply is low at that time, they get paid more for their catch.

How many traps does the average Maine lobsterman haul in a day?

Between 250 and 350.

What is considered a good day's catch?

One pound of lobster per trap, or 250 to 350 pounds.

How many pounds does a successful lobsterman land in a year?

About 20,000 pounds of lobster.

How many pounds do Maine lobstermen collectively land in a year?

Upward of 46 million pounds.

How many working lobstermen are there in Maine?

About 7,000.

How many lobster traps are fished in Maine waters?

More than 3 million.

How many men work a typical Maine lobster boat?

Two—the lobsterman and his sternman. The lobsterman navigates the boat and hauls traps from the ocean floor. The sternman empties the traps and bands the lobsters. Oh, and he rebaits the traps.

He? *He?* Are there any lobsterwomen and sternwomen?

Increasingly, yes. Though lobstering is still a predominately male occupation, there are indeed female lobstermen and sternmen. Often, females come from lobstering families.

What is a highliner?

A lobsterman who consistently brings in the largest catch.

What is a dub?

A lobsterman who
consistently brings in
the smallest catch.

What is a copycat?

A lobsterman who sets
his traps only where a highliner does.

How much power do lobstering families wield?

A lot. To this day, families determine who
fishes where. Rights are passed down from one
generation to the next. Territoriality is key in
lobstering. Violations result in lobster wars.

What's a lobster war?

Also called a gear war, it erupts when intruders
set traps in waters "owned" by other lobstermen.
It can start with one lobsterman tying another's
buoys upside down and escalate to cut lines
and even gunshots.

Why are lobsters banded?

They are cannibalistic and go after other lobsters in tanks, not to mention the fingers of the humans who reach in to pull them out.

How can a rubber band the size of a wide wedding ring fit around those big claws?

The lobsterman has a tool, kind of like pliers, to open the band and slip it over the claw.

What's a little trick to get the lobster to close that claw so you can get the band on?

Blow on the claw, and the lobster will close it.

What if the claw really is too big for a band?

A plug is used. This is a small plastic or wooden peg that is pushed in behind the "thumbs" to keep the claw closed. Plugs were used all the time before the advent of rubber bands. Unfortunately, plugs sometimes cause plug rot.

What's plug rot?

A bacterial infection that can form where the plug penetrates the lobster. This is precisely why rubber bands have replaced plugs as the immobilizer of choice.

What's the most common bait used in the lobster trap?

Herring parts. Make that *very ripe* herring parts.

What's the most bizarre bait used in the lobster trap?

Lobstermen have tried blinking lights, bricks, and coffee mugs.

What is a bait bag?

A small mesh bag to hold bait. It hangs in the trap in the section appropriately called the kitchen.

What is a bait bag made of?

Nylon mesh. Lobstermen and their womenfolk used to net ("knit") them out of twine. Nowadays, lobstermen buy them in the fishing-gear store. They can choose between blue ones, orange ones, and yellow ones.

Where does the bait come from?

A dealer supplies it. Sometimes he's the same person who buys the lobsterman's catch at the end of the day. It used to be that the lobsterman had to haul bait in buckets from the bait house on the wharf. Some wharves now have hydraulic winches that lower the bait to the lobster boat.

What comes up in lobster traps besides lobsters?

Seaweed. Sea ravens, conger eels, wolffish, and crabs. More seaweed. Snails, sea fleas, and shrimp. More seaweed. Dogfish, starfish, scallops, cod. Most any small fish. Even sea urchins, also known as "whore's eggs." (Don't you love that name?)

Does the lobsterman throw these other fish back into the sea?

Not necessarily. He is allowed to keep a small part of this bycatch to feed his family. Lobstermen have been known to pop raw scallops into their mouth as a midmorning snack. Crabs are often kept and sold.

How often does a lobsterman wash his boat?

Every day. While he's fishing, he may scoop up seawater in a bucket to flush the deck; this water runs off through holes called scuppers. Back in the harbor at day's end, he washes the boat with a scrub brush and dish detergent, such as Joy or Dawn. Not all cleaners form a lather in salt water, but these will. He may also use an all-purpose cleaner called Pinkstuf.

What custodial chores must a lobsterman do prior to the season's start?

He repairs his traps, paints his buoys, replaces hog rings, attaches new tags, and overhauls his boat.

What custodial chores must a lobsterman do once the season's up and running?

General maintenance of the boat (including an oil change every other week or so), filling her up with gas, replacing damaged buoys, repairing damaged traps, and keeping a logbook of the location of his traps, the size of his catch, and the price it brings in.

What is bottom paint?

It's thick stuff, usually a reddish rust color, that discourages marine pests, such as barnacles, from latching on. Also called antifouling paint, it is applied yearly.

Does a lobsterman smell of fish?

Coming off the dock, probably. After he's taken soap and a scrub brush to himself, nope.

What's high praise from a lobsterman?

"Finest kind."

Gastronomically Speaking

Is eating lobster healthy for you?

Definitely. Lobster is high in HDL (good cholesterol) and contains less than a gram of fat for every three ounces of meat. Of course, if you dunk a chunk of lobster in melted butter. . . .

Is any part of the lobster bad for you?

The intestine—the long black vein that runs through the tail—should be removed before eating the meat. It is, after all, the intestine. We never know for sure what's in it. Other questionable parts, such as the brain and the stomach, just don't taste that good.

What's the red stuff you sometimes find in a lobster tail?

The firm, coral-colored matter is immature, unfertilized eggs, most commonly called roe. Prior to cooking, roe is black. It is perfectly safe to eat and is even considered a delicacy by some. (Not me. I'll pass on this, thanks.)

What's the green stuff?

Called tomalley, it's the liver of the lobster. It, too, is eaten as a delicacy. (I do love this. It reminds me of moist, chopped chicken liver, only green.)

Is there a difference in taste between male and female lobsters?

Males often have larger claws, so if claws are your thing, you may prefer the male. On the other hand, the female produces roe; if this is your thing, you may prefer the female. As for the rest of the beast, there's little difference in taste.

Is there a difference in taste between hard- and soft-shell lobsters?

Though there is less meat in soft-shell lobsters, it is considered sweeter and more tender than the meat in hard-shell lobsters.

If you're eating boiled live lobster, what part should you eat first?

The claws, knuckles, and tail. These are the most meaty parts and should be eaten while they're hot.

Which tastes better— claw meat or tail meat?

Lobster lovers have been fighting over this for years. Truly, it's a matter of personal preference.

If you don't happen to have a cracker for the knuckles and claws, what can you use?

A meat cleaver, a hammer, a pair of pliers, a rock, even a rolling pin (for squeezing thin strips of meat out of the legs).

What's left?

Legs and flippers (at the end of the tail). In the body, there are also small pieces of meat between the cartilage and the gills.

How much meat do you get from a one-pound lobster?

About ⅔ cup.

How much meat do you get from a 1½-pound lobster?

About 1⅓ cups.

Why does a lobster turn red when cooked?

The lobster always has red pigment, though when the critter is alive the red is less noticeable than its green, blue, or brown pigment. The process of cooking destroys those other colors, though, allowing the red to show through.

Do all lobsters turn red when cooked?

All except white lobsters—albinos—
which are truly rare.

Is a blue lobster edible?

Definitely. When cooked, it turns a pinkish red.

Why is lobster so expensive?

Supply and demand.

Why can't the supply be increased by creating lobster farms?

To date, lobsters have proved difficult to raise in captivity. For one thing, when kept in close quarters they cannibalize one another. Second, it takes six to seven years for a lobster to grow to harvesting size. The cost of caring for them all that time is more than the sales price.

After what town is Lobster Newburgh named?

Newburgh, New York.

What are some other traditional lobster dishes?

Boiled live, of course. And baked stuffed. Then there's Lobster Savannah, Lobster Thermidor, and Lobster Fra Diavolo. And lobster chowder and lobster stew. And, of course, lobster salad.

And some newer ones?

Try lobster ravioli, lobster crepes, lobster pizza, lobster pad Thai, and lobster hash.

What is deviled lobster?

Lobster casserole spiced with dry mustard and cayenne pepper.

And lobster ice cream?

Vanilla ice cream with chunks of claw and tail meat. You can find this only at Ben and Bill's Chocolate Emporium in Bar Harbor, Maine.

What's the only dipper that true lobster lovers would ever think of having with their boiled live lobster?

Melted butter.

What do restaurants serve with lobster that they serve with no other food?

A bib.

Barbara Delinsky has written many best-selling novels in the last two decades, including *Coast Road, Flirting with Pete*, and *The Summer I Dared*. Her newest book is *Looking for Peyton Place*. Most of her stories take place in her home territory of New England. She loves communicating with her readers and can be reached at Box 812894, Wellesley, MA 92492-0026 or via her Web site at *www.barbaradelinsky.com*.